DOGO ARGENTINO AND DOGO ARGENTINE

DOGO ARGENTINO COMPLETE GUIDE

Includes Dogo Argentino, Dogo Argentino Puppies, Argentine Dogo, Argentinian Mastiff, Dogo Dog Care, Dogo Breeders, And More!

by Michael Morris

© DYM Worldwide Publishers

© **DYM Worldwide Publishers**

ISBN: 978-1-911355-16-8

Copyright © DYM Worldwide Publishers, 2016

2 Lansdowne Row, Number 240 London W1J 6HL

endorse the views expressed within them. DYM Worldwide Publishers takes no responsibility for, and will not be liable for, the websites being temporarily or being removed from the Internet. The accuracy and completeness of the information provided herein and opinions stated herein are not guaranteed or warranted to produce any particular results, and the advice or strategies, contained herein may not be suitable for every individual. The author, publisher, distributors, and/or affiliates shall not be liable for any loss incurred as a consequence of the use and application, directly or indirectly of any information presented in this work. This publication is designed to provide information in regards to the subject matter covered. The information included in this book has been compiled to give an overview of the topics covered. The information contained in this book has been compiled to provide an overview of the subject. It is not intended as medical advice and should not be construed as such. For a firm diagnosis of any medical conditions you should consult a doctor or veterinarian (as related to animal health). The writer, publisher, distributors, and/or affiliates of this work are not responsible for any damages or negative consequences following any of the treatments or methods highlighted in this book. Website links are for informational purposes only and should not be seen as a personal endorsement; the same applies to any products or services mentioned in this work. The reader should also be aware that although the web links included were correct at the time of writing they may become out of date in the future. Any pricing or currency exchange rate information was accurate at the date of writing but may become out of date in the future. The Author, Publisher, distributors, and/or affiliates assume no responsibility for pricing and currency exchange rates mentioned within this work.

Foreword

Sometimes in life, we speak of rare breeds. Those are the rare instances when something truly extraordinary catches our eye. The first time I laid eyes on a Dogo Argentino, I had one of those moments. A truly majestic animal, with a noble spirit, the Dogo Argentino has many commendable attributes that gain many admirers.

But as noble and rare as this breed is, it doesn't come without its complications. And even if you are an experienced dog owner, you may need some guidance. That's what this book is all about, taking you through every important aspect of what it means to enter into a relationship with one of these lovely dogs.

In this book, you will learn more about

- General history and background of the Dogo Argentino.
- Where to get a Dogo Argentino – and where NOT to.
- Housebreaking your Dogo Argentino.
- Dogo Argentino health and maintenance.
- Dogo Argentino obedience Training.
- And much, much more!

Table of Contents

Introduction- What the Heck Is A Dogo Argentino?

That's a Good Question! Read More to Find Out!

El Dogo Argentino, the Argentino dog, the Argentine Mastiff, or the just plain "bulldog of Argentina", this Dogo Argentino cachorro goes by many names. But whether you are speaking in English or Spanish, this Dogo Argentino amounts to the same thing, a quality pet that has been bred for success!

And once you get your hands on your very own Dogo Argentino puppy, you will realize just how special this breed really is. So special that it often carries a hefty price tag and a unique range of considerations in care.

But regardless of the price, once you see a Dogo Argentino for sale you can't resist picking one up! Because this Argentinean dog is a real sweetheart and is so family-friendly, if the methods in the guide are followed ... this will be certainly the case.

But, if you ever saw the Dogo Argentino fight, you would realize that this dog was created for much more than cuddling on the couch! Because even though this pooch is mucho people friendly, when push comes to shove they can also be incredibly fierce. They also are extremely loyal. If you ever find yourself in need of some Dogo intervention, due to its tenacity and courage, you won't have to wait long for your Dogo Argentino to come to the rescue!

This Argentino will be there in a hurry! Because the Dogo breed was designed to have a very particular temperament; one that makes these Dogo puppies ideal for hunting and yet incredibly adept in the human social environment. These prissy perros (dogs) are always a showstopper to behold, but they do require the proper upbringing!

The dog breed, which came to be known as Dogo Argentino, was the brainchild of Dr. Antonio Nores Martinez. In 1928, the good doctor began experimenting with different breeds of Argentine fighting dogs. The region has a long and dynamic history of raising canine fighters that date all the way back to the colonial period.

Dr. Martinez was a surgeon living in Cordoba, Argentina, where the typical "Cordoba Fighting Dog" was already very tough and strong, but tended to be a bit anti-social, not having the charisma and depth of more socialized hunting dogs that can work in a group. The good Doctor loved the fighting spirit of these old fighting dogs of Argentina, but he sought to infuse this fighting spirit with the social skills of other friendlier breeds including a quiet loyalty that made the animal a cooperative companion.

This sought-after socialization was the main impetus to create the Dogo Argentino hunting dog. It was in an effort to breed this anti-social behavior and loner tendencies out of the dog; Antonio began crossbreeding different breeds of Mastiff, English Bulldog and Bull Terrier together.

The end result of all of this experimentation was a much more palatable companion, an animal that stands in stark contrast with the unstoppable belligerence of its original ancestor the Cordoba Fighting Dog. This particular breed was designed to deliver much more than the reckless aggression of its predecessor. In a testament to this carefully engineered species, it's interesting to note that (partly because of these dangerous traits) the Cordoba Fighting Dog is now extinct, while the Dogo Argentino lives on successfully and is very desired by dog lovers.

Dr. Antonio wanted to create a dog with a unique set of qualities, to do so he experimented with inter-breeding of the following breeds in the 1920s:

- The Cordoba Fighting Dog (as already mentioned)
- The Bulldog
- The Bull Terrier
- The Great Pyrenees Mastiff
- The Boxer
- The Great Dane
- The Irish Wolf Hound

Not all the results were favorable. But, after a few years, Dr. Martinez found candidates who met the behavioral qualities he sought after.

The Dogo Argentino (also known as the Argentinian Mastiff) has some truly noble qualities. These dogs are incredibly loyal and protective of their owners, displaying an incredible level of tenacity and courage when it comes to safeguarding people and property. There is no other dog that I would rather have in my corner if someone ever broke into my house.

Although much of the dog's ferociousness has been tempered, it is still a strong dog that's quite capable of putting up a fight when it is necessary for them to do so. And, if you are looking for a Dogo Argentino cazando, a dog that can catch vermin, these guys won't disappoint in that area either.

For its size the Dogo is amazingly light on its feet, as quick as a cat, these dogs can ferret out rats, mice or just about any other nuisance that comes your way. As you can see, Dr. Antonio truly did a truly great service in creating a perfect balance of fighting dog and lovable puppy. Yes, his work has resulted in the Argentine Mastiff which began to rise rapidly in popularity within Argentina and worldwide.

Chapter 1-The Argentine Dogo, A Very Unique Personality.

Get Acquainted with Your Dogo

As mentioned, because of the personality types at play from its originating breeds, the Dogo Argentino temperament is very unique. Everything about this dog is special, and its own unique perspective and attitude are no different. So, prior to committing yourself to your own Dogo Argentino and visiting breeders, you should take the time to get yourself acquainted with exactly what this dog is and what it has to offer.

One of the most important things to realize about this breed is that they are highly social animals, and they naturally gravitate toward being a pack leader. If no one around them—human or animal—is taking on that role as the leader, they will then automatically volunteer themselves into that role!

Structure and Order

This is why proper training from a young age is so important for your Dogo Argentino. As we will discuss in greater depth in the next chapter of this book, if you want to train your Dogo successfully you have to do it early on. Your Dogo needs strong and firm direction from the beginning; this is crucial to ensure a healthy relationship!

It is for this reason that it is often not recommended for first-time dog owners to take on the task of instructing the Dogo Argentino. These strong-willed dogs need their owner to create clear boundaries and order. If you cannot provide the right structure the Dogo personality needs, any hope of successfully training him will be an unlikely prospect.

Dogo Argentino is fully capable of being your most diligent disciple, but their desire for obedience only kicks in if you provide the appropriate structure for them to thrive in. This breed naturally gravitates toward a leader, and if you don't present yourself as a leader with real authority from the get go, they will ultimately look somewhere else for their leadership.

The Dogo Argentino is very intelligent, with a personality that is eager to impress others with its ability to follow the rules, but it can only do this need if there are well-structured rules for it to follow. So anyone training this dog will have to create an adequate learning environment and social structure for them from when they are just puppies .

If you are insecure about your own training skills, don't hesitate to reach out to a professional. If this means contacting a local dog trainer or even enrolling your Dogo in a puppy pre-school course, don't hesitate. Once they move past this puppy stage of their life, most of their behavior and life-patterns are already set.

Early and Often Boundary Setting is Key

This is why I can't stress enough the need to train these animals at a young age, because although they are fully capable of learning obedience if you don't teach them early they can become quite aggressive and dangerous. Your Dogos personality begins to take shape as a pup, and if proper social norms are not instilled at this pivotal stage, his social skills may be permanently maligned.

We will cover the full aspects of proper socialization techniques and obedience training in much more depth in further chapters of this text. So if you are serious and committed to raising a well-mannered Dogo, by all means, please purchase the full edition of this book so that you know how to avoid the unpleasant situation of an out of control and aggressive Dogo.

The Dogo as a Family Friendly Companion

Under the right conditions, one aspect of the Dogo Argentino's unique personality that works to benefit families is how well it does with children. Dogo Argentinos love kids, and the more energy the children have, the more energy the dog has. This is, of course, assuming the dog is well-balanced in its demeanor and well-trained from an early age to respect boundaries.

But take this enthusiasm with a grain of salt, because while the Dogo Argentino can be protective and caring for the children in your household, those that your dog deems to be outside of its own pack, (including other neighborhood children), your dog could exhibit signs of territorial aggression. So you must be very cautious to both socialize your Dogo as mentioned below, as well as always supervise any play with children.

This is yet another reason why it is so important to have the Dogo socialized early on. It will prevent any external aggression to other children or animals in the neighborhood. The Dogo has a loyal personality, but you need to help him understand that this loyalty to you and your immediate family should not transform into instant aggression for those outside of your immediate circle.

Your Dogos territorial leanings and protectiveness aside, however, most of the time kids can't help but love these guys simply for the fact that they never get tired of playing! These dogs tend to match up their energy level with those around them, making them the perfect playmate of a hyperactive child. They just love to goof off and roughhouse.

But at the same time, if everyone around them is quiet and subdued, this Dogo will ultimately follow suit. Because although these dogs have an endless supply of energy, they also have a personal drive toward obedience. It is this overwhelming desire to follow the rules set down by their pack leader, (that's you / or whom you nominate in your household), that they exert immense self-control in order to attain this subservience to the household leader.

These dogs are also always alert; watching out for the inner and outer workings of the family. This makes them the perfect watch dog. It is this aspect of the Dogos personality that can work as a double-edged sword, however, and as mentioned earlier, it is this precisely this protective temperament of the Dogo that tends to make them rather territorial in nature.

In order to prevent them from acting on these deep-seated tendencies in their personality, and to keep them from barking at houseguests and neighbors, they have to be trained to be accepting of others in the neighborhood. This is why proper socialization during the puppy stage is so vital. So what are you waiting for? Read this book to find out more!

Chapter 2-Dogo Argentino Puppies! How Much Is That Dogo Argentino In The Window?

Dogo Argentino for Sale!

So, you would like to buy a Dogo Argentino? Even at the most affordable of Dogo Argentino kennels, this dog can run anywhere from $500 to $1500 / (€450 to €1350), making the financial component alone, enough to ensure at least a rudimentary amount of commitment on the part of a buyer. No one forks over that much cash without at least some idea of what he or she might be getting into.

Before you can even buy a Dogo, you are usually placed on a waiting list. In many cases, you are waitlisted for Dogos that are not even born yet. And, if you are purchasing your dog from outside the United States you may have to wait up to six months while your Dogo is in Quarantine.

Countries Which Restrict or Ban the Dogo Argentino

Some countries and some municipalities totally ban (rare) or restrict (more common) the Dogo Argentino breed. This is not unique to the Dogo Argentino as a breed; it usually affects breeds based on its fighting dog ancestor.

The countries as of this writing that restrict or ban the breed are below. If you live in one of these countries please carefully check all such rules yourself, in addition as they do change from time to time:

- **Australia** (Restrictions: None may be imported. Other restrictions vary by state including insurance, sterilization, muzzling, leashes, selling, etc. Please check with your state).

- **Bermuda** (Banned! No import or ownership subject to penalties if violated).

- **Israel** (Restrictions: No Imports at all. Dogs must be muzzled and on leash in public.)

- **Italy** (Restrictions: All owners must take special care for leash and muzzle, though this applies to all dogs).

- **Malta** (Restrictions, please see local laws for more clarity.

- **New Zealand** (Restrictions: You can own but mandatory microchipping. You must also sterilize as well as use short leashes and muzzles at all times in public.

- **Norway** (Banned! Civil and or criminal penalties apply.)

- **Portugal** (Banned, cannot be kept.)

- **Romania** (Restrictions on possession of the breed to those over 18, psychological and judicial screening process required for the owner).

- **Singapore** (Restrictions: sterilization, microchipping, insurance of $100, 000 SGD, dog must be kept on a short leash and with a muzzle in public places)

- **Spain** (Restrictions: can be kept with heavy restrictions; license required, criminal record check for the owner, mental and physical check, liability insurance).

- **The UK** (Banned! Ban on owning, cultivation, sale, purchase, exchange. Illegal to own with penalties of £5,000 and/or 6 months imprisonment.

- **Turkey** (Restrictions: No sale, purchase, advertising, or exchange. Fines of 2,500 – 3,500 Lira if violated).

- **Ukraine** (Restrictions: insurance, microchipping, walking on a short leash and muzzle are obligatory).

- **USA** – (Possible Restrictions. Certain local municipalities have put into place restrictions; please check with your local city, county, and state for more information to be assured you are able to keep the breed or which restrictions you need to follow. The United States has no nationwide bans on any breed).

If you live in one of these countries or plan to live in one of them soon, check the latest rules before investing in a Dogo Argentino! No matter where you live please ensure to abide by your local laws 100% when it comes to dog ownership.

Quarantine Laws

It varies by country, but the "Quarantine Laws" — as they are called — are dependent on the local ordinance of where you live. These regulations are put in place on dogs imported from outside the country to take the time to make sure that the dog has all of its required vaccinations and is in sound health and is not a threat to the existing animal population.

Many potential Dogo owners take all this extra time to take complete stock of their finances and exactly how much their new Dogo is going to cost them. Getting on a waiting list indicates dedication and preparation for the special animal that is about to share your home with you.

During this time, you should read as many books as you can to familiarize yourself with the time and monetary investment that it takes to be a successful Dogo owner.

Time Investment?

There are only 24 hours in a day, and no matter what we do we can't change that. Having that said. Before we consider bringing a Dogo Argentino into our lives, we need to make sure that we are able to invest enough time with it so that the Dogo has the quality of life that he deserves.

Many of us might be more than ready to open up our pocketbook to invest our money, but finances aside, your true investment is going to be your time. This dog needs your loving time and commitment in order for him to be healthy and trained.

As we discussed in the previous chapter, the Dogo generally has a good disposition, but he also has a lot of energy. So, it would be a shame if you purchased this breed only to leave him locked up all day long in your apartment.

Don't get me wrong; these animals can do just fine in an apartment or smaller home setting, **but only if you**

provide them with enough exercise to channel out some of their energy. The Dogo Argentino wasn't made for inaction and needs a time and place where it can freely roam and exercise.

This can be accomplished either through having a big yard or garden for the Dogo to be fenced in during the day or if you live in a tiny apartment, simply make the time to take the dog out on really long walks for exercise.

As you can see, a Dogo Argentino is not just an investment of your money, but also an investment of your time. If you don't already have one, or a workable combination of the two energy releasing solutions mentioned in the above paragraph, you might want to reconsider buying the dynamo that is our Dogo.

Where can you Find a Dogo Argentino?

Now that we have gotten this little prerequisite out of the way, let's focus on just where you might be able to find your very own Dogo Argentino.

Since your Dogo comes from such a rare and refined breed, you may need to start off your search by contacting a "breed club". And if you live anywhere in North America one of the best places that you could go to is the "American Kennel Club".

The AKC is the largest dog breeding organization in the United States. The American Kennel Club is responsible for maintaining most breed standards in the region. In order for a purebred puppy to be officially registered with the American Kennel Club, the dog's parents must be registered as well.

Documenting the dog's ancestry back to its parents is a tremendous help in understanding the kind of dog you are purchasing. The best and most immediate, way to know whether or not your Dogo will be a good match for you is to meet your little puppies parents. A thorough breeder like the AKC recommends provides you the opportunity to do just that.

The American Kennel Club is probably the most renowned point of contact you can find in North America, so feel free to visit them at http://www.akc.org to take your first step in finding
your Dogo.

This site is very informative, always giving a daily calendar of events searchable by the area where you live. From here you can obtain the contact information of individual breeders. You can use it to keep in contact with breeders by phone and e-mail until your purchase has been made.

Make sure that your breeder keeps you updated about potential litters of puppies and how many each litter currently has available. The number of pups left in a litter is important to take note since the leftover pups can usually be sold at a
discount price.

There is no real basis to make the last of the litter undesirable, but even so, it is generally quite common for the breeder to discount the last few puppies of his litter. If this is the case, this is a discount that you might as well take them up on.

Many potential buyers are often afraid that the last dog of the litter is the weak "runt of the litter" but this is a myth. Sometimes the last pick is simply the last pick, and the last pick is likely not much better or worse than the first pick.

The only thing different is the money that you might save! So yes, be sure and take your breeder up on a possible discount if you are left with the last of the litter!

Even cheaper than the discounted last pick of the litter would be a Dogo puppy that is completely free. This may seem unlikely due to the hefty price tag usually associated with this breed, but just like every other dog in existence, the Argentine Dogo can, in fact, be found at shelters and Rescue Organizations.

You may need to do some detective work, but if you research all the options in your area, you just might hit pay dirt and gain a great Dogo for next to nothing. Rescue shelters in particular, often specialize in these breeds and can offer you an excellent opportunity for acquiring your Dogo.

And as the Dogo has gained in popularity, quite a following has developed in the rescue circuit for it. In fact, you can find out all you ever wanted to know by simply going online and searching for the **"Dogo Argentino Rescue Network,"** or as it is known by its somewhat goofy acronym, "DARN." Here you will find the ultimate resource in Dogo Argentino rescue. Search on Facebook for its latest link; it's easy to find.

Rescue dogs sometimes carry the stigma of being defective or of being the dog's people rejected because they had some kind of problem. More often than not, though, the dog is really just fine, and it was only the owner that had a problem.

Many times people get a Dogo and are simply unprepared for the responsibility of raising them, and so they quickly rid themselves of the animal by dumping them onto a rescue shelter.

People have both changed their minds and lifestyles that cause them to give up their dogs, and the actions of the Dogo has little to do with the outcome. So the idea that rescue dogs are all, somehow, inherently defective is false.

Health Issues with Some Dogo Puppies or Adults

That is not to say, however, that all of the Dogos at a rescue will be without health problems. However, there are always a few cases of owners who abandon their dogs because they do find some sort of genetic flaw or abnormality.

With the Dogo Argentino, the most common instance of this rejection occurs when a Dogo is found to be deaf. Because deafness, as we will discuss later in this book, is the most common genetic defect that Dogos suffer from. For some owners when they find out that their animal is deaf, they often give their dog up to the rescue shelter.

But even if some of them are deaf, what they may lack in hearing they make up with love, and for someone who can look past their disability they are still one of the most loving and fun dog's you could ever have! So please don't give up on these guys so easily. Regardless of any blemish, find the dog that best fits for you.

I recently heard of a rather heartwarming story about a family that took in a rescue Dogo. This Dogo Argentino had seen the darker side of life, being repeatedly subjected to dog fighting and abuse.

He even had the horrific experience of being used as a bait dog, a situation in which a dog is placed out in the center of a fight to lure out the other dogs, truly disturbing.

By the time the police shut this horrid enterprise down this Dogo was in rough shape. One of his ears had been completely torn off; he had scars all over his body and a gaping wound on his side.

He couldn't be in worse shape, and when he was dropped off at the rescue shelter, his prognosis was not good. But this Dogo was special, and he had a will not only to survive but to thrive.

After a few months of proper rest and nutrition at this rescue shelter, he improved dramatically. With the basics of his health taken care of, he became the happiest Dogo at the shelter. He soon became a favorite, and it wasn't long before a family gladly adopted the friendly pooch.

If this Dogo could rise above his terrible circumstances, it's clearly possible for any Dogo in rescue to be given a second life. So don't hesitate to adopt a Dogo from your local rescue shelter and give him the home he deserves.

The other great advantage of adopting any dog is usually that they are a little older and already been broken in. So although people love the cuteness of puppies, you should seriously consider adopting a fully grown Argentine mastiff that already knows what to do instead. That way you can save a lot of time (and stress) by getting a dog that is already trained in the basics.

Of all the methods of obtaining a Dogo Argentino, contacting a breeder is probably your safest bet. Next to direct contact with a breeder, locating a rescue service specifically devoted to Dogo Argentino's is the next best.

Both of these methods of acquisition will undoubtedly offer you some sense of certainty in the animal's health and general wellbeing. With any other method, your animal's background may not be quite as well guaranteed.

Why I Don't Recommend Pet Stores For Finding Your Dogo Puppy

Pet Stores are often a popular choice, but even if you manage to find a seemingly healthy Dogo at your local pet shop, there is no guarantee about the Dogos actual health. Pet stores are by no means as thorough in their selection process as a professional breeder or kennel.

Pet stores tend to rely on impulse buys. Seeking to literally put your Dogo for sale, right there in the window, so that when you just happen to glance at the animal, you are moved to buy it, no questions asked.

This is the marketing tactic used in commercial Pet Stores. I'm not saying that it's impossible to find a good Dogo at a Pet Store, but buyers beware! The guarantee from a Pet Store is just not there.

Most Pet Stores do not screen the parents of the Dogo and have no way of knowing the genetic history and future potential of health problems for the animals. This is why most serious Dogo buyers wouldn't even darken a Pet Store door.

The other downside of Pet Stores is the negative connotation most of them carry as being nothing more than commercialized puppy mills. With animals spending their entire life in a cage, untrained, barely socialized and never even seeing carpet, let alone grass, giving them no clue as to what their future life with you may be like.

This is a much less ideal situation than the much more caring and structured environment that breeders and kennels provide. And while a Pet Store offers a very limited guarantee, when we move beyond Pet Stores, Kennels, and Breeders completely, we are really going for a wild card.

Sure anyone can put an advertisement up in the newspaper claiming to have purebred Dogo Pups, but you are really only taking their word for it. Even if they claim to have the dog's complete pedigree, without recognition by an official organization such as the AKC, this documentation is rather meaningless.

Craig's List (http://www.craigslist.com) and other online, as well as offline, classified ad sources sometimes contain offers to sell Dogos on a daily basis. But in utilizing a resource such as this, you are really going "off the grid" and into the dark.

So if you think you have found a good deal from an off the grid Dogo seller such as this, just be careful. And take it with a grain of salt whenever your eyes come across that excited proclamation, "Dogo Argentino For Sale!"

Chapter 3-Dogo Argentino
House Training

Establishing a Solid Routine

No matter what kind of dog you may have, house training is never the most exciting of tasks. But breaking in your Dogo Argentino shouldn't be too difficult as long as you start them out with ample structure and guidance.

Because even though the Dogo has at times what can be described as a rather forceful personality, the dog's primary drive is for obedience. So once you set down clear guidelines, in regard to the Dogos potty training, the dog will strive to abide by them.

You really want to avoid confusing your Dogo, this will only make for a stressful, or even worse, a fearful event. Making the Argentine Mastiff fearful is to be avoided at all cost, because once potty training becomes a frightful ordeal, your Dogo pup may begin to freeze up and decide that it's just too scary to relieve itself in front of you.

Due to such fearful associations, your dog may then opt to go when (and where) you aren't looking. So if you don't want to wake up at 6 in the morning to step in something at the foot of your bed that isn't the morning newspaper, then we better get this right!

In order to develop a solid schedule with your Dogo, you should always begin the puppy's day, as soon as it wakes up, taking it out the door for a walk. Then, take it out at least four more times after this: taking him out twice during midday and two more times in the evening.

Mastering your Argentinian Mastiff with Positi Reinforcement

Along with these designated bathroom times, it's also important to be on the lookout for your dog's own signs and signals of a sudden urge to go, such as suddenly circling or vigorously sniffing the floor. This is a clear indication that the animal is looking for a place to relieve itself. So as soon as you see that, get your Dogo outside.

Just to let your puppy know that these trips outside have to be taken seriously, make them short and to the point. If your Dogo does not begin to relieve itself within the first few minutes of the walk, take him back inside.

This teaches the dog not to waste your time, making him realize that if it doesn't use the opportunity you give him to relieve itself, he will have to go back inside and wait for the next time.

If the Dogo does successfully relieve itself, however, you should not miss the opportunity to let your Dogo know that what he did was a good thing. As soon as your Dogo finishes, you should congratulate him with a pleasant confirmation such as, "Good Dog!"

This affirmation is all your Dogo is looking for, and it serves to let the puppy know that it succeeded in the obedience that it is ultimately seeking.

If, of course, your dog starts to throw off the cues of really needing to go outside—by circling/sniffing—by all means take him out, but even so, always make your trips short so the Dogo knows that going outside in these instances is primarily for relief and should be treated as such.

This way it is firmly established to the puppy that going outside during these designated periods is a time for the relief of its bodily functions, not a time to play around.

Another thing that you should keep in mind is that you should always ask your dog before you take him out. You might be thinking, "What ask my dog? He doesn't understand me?" Why would I ask?"

You may be right that the dog is unable to comprehend the exact phonetics of your language, but your Dogo can most certainly master the meaning behind certain tones and sounds and learn to associate them with different tasks and requests.

So developing a key phrase for your puppy that signifies bathroom breaks is an excellent administrative and reinforcement tool that can be used very early on in your dog's progress. To get my own dog's ready to go, I usually ask them plain and straightforward, "Want to go outside?" or even the abbreviated, "Go outside?"

I can tell you, they may not know you are referencing the great outdoors exactly, but do it enough before you take your animal to relieve itself, and it will most definitely associate the phrase with going to the bathroom.

Amazingly posing this task as a question will allow your Dogo the chance to think about whether or not it really needs to go outside. If your Dogo needs to go out, it won't hide it.

If your Dogo needs to go outside, upon hearing the cue for a bathroom break he will get a burst of energy—and after a few wags of the tail as confirmation—will start heading toward the door like clockwork.

Alternative Potty Reinforcement for your Argentine Mastiff

"But why does the Potty have to always be outside? Sometimes I want to bring the Potty Indoors!"

If, however, after all is said and done, you are still having a particularly hard time getting your puppy to adhere to the potty schedule, as a temporary means of transition, you could resort to what are known as "potty pads." These potty pads work by being chemically treated with a scent that makes the dog want to do its doo-doo on them.

This works well as a good transition, because although the dog may not be going outside, they are still being conditioned only to use the bathroom in a designated area: on the pad.

Because as we've already stressed in this book, in the end, it is all about structure, and if something such as a potty pad provides your Dogo its first semblance of structured potty training, don't hesitate to use it.

But while a designated pad could prove to be a useful transitional tool, only default to the chemically treated pads, do not attempt to use any non-treated surface in replace of these. Some owner's try to substitute the potty pads for newspaper and this is only a recipe for failure.

Because without the special chemical signature of a potty pad, even though a patch of newspaper may look like a designated spot to you, to your Argentine Mastiff it just looks like everything else.

If your Dogo does not smell the special chemical tags of the potty pad, it has no way to differentiate a newspaper surface from a carpet surface, and so the end result of this would be one very confused Dogo who starts relieving itself all over the place.

So in order to prevent a puppy from having a potty free-for-all based on confusion, you must transition your Dogo. Stick to the chemically-treated potty pads that were specially designed for the task at hand.

Further House Training Tips for Your Dogo

"Yes, It's that Important!"

But for the times that you do manage to walk your dog outside and he successfully goes to the bathroom, I have one more piece of advice for you. Make sure your Dogo is clean before he goes back inside! Because when your pup, just like a human child, is still learning the ropes when it comes to potty training, he doesn't always manage to clean himself properly.

This was a lesson that my wife and I learned all too clearly when we first got our own Dogo puppy. I still remember the day that our pooch gave us a bathroom training surprise. We had just finished a fairly productive walk, and we were happy that our Dogo had seemingly completed the task of relieving himself. So glad, it seemed, that we hadn't checked him to make sure he was clean when we went inside the house! It wasn't long though after I plopped down on the couch in the living room when my wife suddenly looked at me and asked, "What's that smell?"

Her nose is always a bit quicker than mine and, at first, I was a bit confused at the line of questioning and comically responded, "Well, it's not me!" But as soon as I replied, the odor she was referring to finally hit me. I looked over at the Dogo sitting next to me and realize it's coming from him.

At this point, our Dogo puppy is happily prancing around on the couch oblivious to his slinkiness. When I looked down, I saw the exact source of the odor. Somehow our dog has the remnants of a big piece of kaka smeared all over his right front paw.

Whether he stepped in his own mess or another dog's we weren't sure, but all we knew was that if we didn't get this dog out the door in a hurry, he was about to smear his poopy footprints all over the house! So without saying a word, I grabbed the Dogo and bolted to the door, with my wife following frantically behind.

She then turned on the outdoor hose as I tried to hold the hyper doggy in place. We were fortunate enough to be able to catch him before he did any real damage. A word to the wise, when you are potty training your Dogo, you better check him at the door!

After the experience we had with our Dogo, we made it a rule to take the time to inspect his paws before we go inside. I began to make myself stop at the door, and then after wiping my own feet on the doormat; I would then turn to the Dogo to check out if he had any unsightly remnants left on his feet.

These dogs, being the great imitators they are, however, began to get the idea of what I was doing and comically enough started wiping his own paws right after I wiped my feet.

Above all, potty training your Dogo Argentino is going to take patience and perseverance. No matter how many times your Dogo stumbles, just take it in stride, and keep your dog on a solid routine.

Follow these steps and you and your Dogos potty training experience will be a relatively stress-free and productive one. Now be proud that your Dogo has ceased messing up your house and graduated on to better things.

Chapter 4-The Dogo Diet

Dogo Argentino Breeders to the Feeders. What should I feed my Dogo Argentino?

So your puppy is getting a little older, and you want to know what's best to feed the little guy as he starts to grow? Well, you came to the right place; because, in this chapter, we will teach you how to feed your Dogos Argentino properly!

No, you don't have to feed him fine Argentinean food in order for this pooch to be healthy, but you do want him to have a good basic diet to get started with.

If you are getting your Dogo from a breeder, the dog should already be weaned from its mother's milk by the time you get it. Allowing your Dogo to ingest the nutrients in mother's milk during its infancy will prove very beneficial later on during the course of its life.

The mother's milk is the best multi-vitamin or supplement that your puppy could ever get a hold of, building the dog's immune system and even determining the Dogos future potential for growth.

So the first objective of any Dogo diet plan is to make sure that the animal has been properly weaned. It typically takes about eight weeks for a Dogo to be completely weaned from its mother. Once this has been done, you can then move onto a variety of options for starter food for the puppy.

One of the most common—and most economically priced dog food to feed your Dogo is going to be a primarily grain-based. Grained-based foods tend to consist of a soy-based protein.

While this kind of protein does wonders in building muscle in your Dogo, it also has the rather unpleasant side effect of creating excess flatulence in your dog. This is an aspect of this diet that can be both unpleasant, and embarrassing.

I learned this the hard way with one of my own Dogos. had been feeding the dog the same brand of food for a while but then one day when I was at the local pet store to stock up, I caught sight of a new dry, soy protein-based brand.

It was cheaper, so I thought I would give it a shot. Well, folks, let me just say that after my dog spent just a few days on this new food, the nature trail at my local park will never be the same!

I think my Dogo and I made a permanent impression on that place! I was taking him around the dog path when I suddenly heard a thunderous rumble coming from my Dogos stomach.

I never knew that dogs could have such a noisy tummy, but I just shrugged and took him on down the path. He stopped because he seemed interested in some brush on the side of the trail, a potential place for him to do his business, or so I thought. So, I stopped and let him do it.

That's when this family of bicycle riders, I mean the whole family -- dad on the first bike, and mom following behind towing her toddler daughter in a ride-along bike carriage, all came riding by.

Well, while my Dogo was sniffing away at the ground and shrubbery in front of him, I decided to be friendly and waved at the approaching family.

The man and woman both smiled and waved back, and the whole family then slowed down as they glided by. And then right when the woman's bike passed within inches of me, with the riders looking straight ahead, my Dogo let out the loudest, raunchiest, dirtiest explosion I had ever heard!

I didn't even know dogs could make gastronomical sounds like that! You just don't expect a dog to blast out gas in such a manner, and neither did that family riding by. The woman spun her head around facing me instantly as her jaw dropped. She had a look of contempt and disgust on his face.

The man then turned his head, and looked as if he was going to kill me! The look of condemnation was so complete I thought he was about to shout, "How dare you ambush my family with that!"

But fortunately, my Dogo was not through yet and now with everyone watching he ripped out another one just in time to vindicate me. The man's look of rage then quickly shifted to astonishment as he sputtered, "What? Is that's your dog farting like that?"

The biking family then rode off to leave me and my Dogo embarrassed and ashamed. But as they left, the woman gave one last piece of parting advice, "Be careful what you feed that thing!"

Yes, indeed! And that is the purpose of my little testimony; a Dogos digestive tract can be very sensitive, so yes, you gotta be careful what you feed him. If your dog starts having gas or any other sign of indigestion, don't hesitate to change diets.

Special Additions to the Dogo Argentino Diet

All dogs, like people, are slightly different. So, in celebration of this diversity, we have to realize that some may require special variations to their diet. If your Dogo seems to be having a hard time with his normal dog food, then don't hesitate to take the little guy to the vet to be checked out. After taking a close look at your doggy's tummy, he might recommend a special diet to help provide him with what he needs.

Besides making certain your dog doesn't suffer from the above-mentioned indigestion, the food that you feed your Dogo will also have an immediate impact on your dog's coat and even his temperament. In my own experience, I have found that Purina's classic Alpo dog food can do wonders for a Dogo.

It's a widely available brand that you can find at just about any grocery store, but this stuff really is packed with a good balance of proteins, vitamins, and minerals; generally providing your Dogo with everything he needs; nothing more and nothing less.

Because unlike some other newer Purina brands on the market such as "Beneful," regardless of what the name might imply, your Dogo may not receive the right kind of Benefit. This is because many of these newer brands of dog food kibble contain quite a bit of unnecessary filler in their ingredients.

One of the most worrisome of these extra ingredients is that of a little something called, "propylene glycol." Remember the name and check your dog food brand to see if it contains it because propylene glycol has been known to create some serious side effects in many of the dogs that consume it.

Propylene Glycol is actually a form of fermented alcohol, and it has been used in everything from paint, varnish, and even anti-freeze. You may be wondering why an ingredient found in anti-freeze would be in dog food at all.

Dogo Argentino and Argentine Dogo | 46

But, believe it or not, this element is FDA approved in small doses for general consumption.

My First Criteria: "Is it Food?"

But despite FDA approval, there are currently many lawsuits for dog's that have suffered seizures and even death from prolonged consumption of dog food containing Propylene Glycol. Even if this compound remains completely harmless for most dogs, I would really hate to win the unlucky lottery and have one of the few Dogos that have a deadly reaction.

This is why I stick to Purina's classic Alpo formula that does not contain Propylene Glycol. Alpo consists of a ground yellow corn base with soybean meal. Alpo will provide your Dogo with its daily protein and calcium requirements as well as vital Vitamin B-12, and Vitamin D supplements necessary for your Dogos health and proper digestion.

The Great Dogo Diet Debate. Wet or Dry Dogfood?

Wet Food...Dry Food... I don't really care...
As long as you do the dishes!

Beyond picking your own particular brand of dog food, one of the bigger debates raging around your Dogos diet is whether to feed him wet or dry food. When we say wet food we are referring to the moist dog food mixture that comes out of a can, whereas the dry variety which is known as "kibble" comes in a paper bag.

Some swear by canned food while others swear by the dry. While both kinds can be adequately nutritious for your dog's diet, wet, canned foods can cause some undesired effects in your animal. Some Dogos suffer from diarrhea after being introduced to wet food while many others develop behavioral issues due to their strong craving for the canned food.

Dog's undoubtedly love canned dog food, and it most certainly must taste good for them. But, just be warned once you feed these tasty morsels to your Dogo it can be very hard to wean them off of it. Although the soft, wet food is tasty to your dog, it doesn't provide some of the benefits that dry kibble will provide for them later on in their lives.

One of the main advantages of having your dog consume dry kibble is the fact that, while their wet canned food probably just gets stuck in their teeth, —dry kibble actually helps them clean their teeth.

This kind of food is specially made to help strengthen and clean your Dogos teeth as he happily crunches and munches on the kibble. This is of particular importance as your Dogo gets older. When your dog eats soft food its whole life its teeth will seriously deteriorate from their lack of the influence and use of dry food.

The only real advantage of wet food is if you have an extremely finicky eater. The great taste of canned food is usually all you need to coax your dog into eating it. But, if you can get your dog to eat dry food, it is recommended that you get your Dogo to start out on a dry kibble regimen first before you introduce it to anything else.

Wet dog food should be used only as the exception and not the rule. So unless your animal has an extreme aversion to dry kibble, get him started on dry dog food as his food base early on in his life.

Dry food always comes in many different flavors too, so if your Dogo seems a little bored with his kibble, you can always switch it to a different flavor for him with the same brand of dry food.

Transitioning Your Meal Plans Over Time

Beyond consistency with the type of dog food you use, you should also keep your Dogos feeding times consistent. At about eight weeks old your Dogo should be fed twice a day; ideally, you should be feeding him in the morning and in the evening.

Once your dog has stopped growing and reached the adult marker of 12-18 months, you then need to consider decreasing the amount of food you feed your dog. As he moves into his next stage of life, you need to be ready to change his meal plan to reflect his changing needs as an adult Dogo.

As an adult, your Dogo at this point no longer needs all of that extra protein and calcium for growing muscles and bones. Therefore, in order to prevent your dog from gaining weight as an adult, his diet needs to be decreased. It's the simple caloric law we all face; that equates are body weight to being dependent on a number of calories we consume versus how many we burn.

As an adult, your dog's metabolism will slow down making it harder for him to break down calories and increasing the risk of obesity. Yes, just like us human beings, the Dogos metabolism slows with age.

To avoid complications of weight gain, as your dog approaches middle age, you may want to reduce his diet to one generous bowl of dog food a day. Or, you might try decreasing the amount of food in each of his daily rations. That way you can ensure that your Dogo maintains an excellent and healthy diet for the rest of his life.

Chapter 5-Tempering Your Dogo Argentino's Temperament! Teach That Dogo Obedience

"Like my Momma Dogo Used to Always Say, 'Be A Good Dogo and the Rest Will Follow!"

Your Dogo Argentino Needs Positive Reinforcement to Thrive

The only two things that you really need to begin training your Dogo is an ample supply of treats and your dog's unbridled attention. And fortunately, since your dog's heart is most likely in his stomach much of the time, if you have one component of this obedience equation you will invariably end up with the other.

Treats are used as an initial incentive to get your Dogo to focus and do what you want him to do. The treat is the tool that gets you dog's attention to cooperate with training and helps to wire his brain to associate the training you guided him toward as a good behavior that he will be rewarded for performing.

Along with food, you should also couple your treat giving with positive affirmations of your dog's good behavior. This way as you hand out the treat and the dog gets a bit of a dopamine rush in his head for being rewarded. You just gotta love those reward centers that nature gave us! You also must reinforce the good feeling he has with your own signature comments such as, 'Good dog!"

This way, your animal will associate both the treat and your positive feedback with the good feeling it gets when it does something you want him to do. In that way, you don't necessarily always have to give a treat just to get your dog to do something worthwhile, and your dog will learn to be happy to do what it is instructed to do just in order to seek your praise and goodwill.

Since the Dogo Argentino is a dog that naturally seeks to please the leader of its pack, it will soon thrive on your pats on the back and praises of approval. This allows your dog to be an active learner and feel rewarded while acquiring valuable skills.

The Rosetta Stone: Teaching Your Dogo to Sit!

"Really? That's what all you want? Sit on my Butt? Ok!"

Probably the most important thing you can teach your Dogo is to sit. If your Dogo knows nothing else and is bouncing off the walls, wreaking havoc and doing everything else wrong. if you can at least get him to understand your command of "Sit" you will instantly be able to neutralize his hyperactive behavior.

So, even if he's in the midst of barking at the neighbors, rummaging through the trashcan, or attempting to eat the family cat, if he understands this one basic command he will most like stop everything he is doing in order to sit down for you.

The training process should involve all of your Dogos senses. Teaching him to 'Sit' is the perfect example of that. First, get your dog's attention with the sound of your voice and then once he is looking your way you take out the treat and start working on your Dogos visual cues.

As he sees the treat right in front of him, his mind will start going into overdrive wondering what you are about to offer him.

Now bring in the dog's most overpowering sense of all, his sense of smell by hanging the treat right over his nose, and allow him to get a good whiff of it in your hand. Your dog will most likely rise up and try to take the treat, as he rises quickly withdraw your hand and give a guiding command with a negative preface, tell him, "No... Sit!"

At this point, you have your dog in a position to where he is trying to figure out what you want him to do. Your dog is wondering what you mean by withdrawing the tasty treat and then barking out that strange new word "Sit." Wait a moment while your dog thinks this one through and then bring the treat back out as you once again command with even more force, "Sit!"

At this point, you have your Dogos undivided attention, and he is no doubt staring at you trying to figure out what in the heck you are trying to tell him. He's may be unsure what to do yet, but he is trying his best to figure it out, looking at you for any clue you can give.

It is in this indecisive state that you will help him out a bit. While he's staring at you, still unsure what to do, take the treat and hold it directly over the dog's head so that he has to look directly up in order to keep the treat in his line of sight.

With the dog in this position with his knees bending back and his neck angling up struggling to keep his eyes on the prize, he will be much more inclined actually to sit down to get a better look. This is the obedience trick you have up your sleeves, and without him even realizing it you can get your Dogo to follow your lead by mere coincidence.

Almost by chance, your pooch will most likely sit down just to keep track of the dangling food, and when he does sit down get ready to shower him with praise by not only giving him the treat but also giving him some love.

This is a happy moment for you that your dog has (even inadvertently) listened to your command so let your Dogo know you are pleased by affectionately patting his back and telling him, "Yes, sit! Good boy! Good dog!"

You can give yourself a pat on the back too, because after this bit of struggle your dog has now discovered the Rosetta stone that will unlock his complete understanding of all your commands. Now that he has come to grips with what, "Sit" means you can use this as your starting point to teach him every other command you can think of.

But, what I would really recommend in expanding his vocabulary of obedience is to teach your Dogo simply to 'Come' to you in the first place. Because when you are in a real pinch, such as when you are in a public place, and your dog is wandering too far for you to catch, being able to command your dog to come back to you is crucial.

This is usually most easily accomplished by shouting out the simple one-word phrase of "come." As you issue, this command make sure that you stay in a positive disposition. Don't yell at your Dogo harshly, but keep your voice and facial expression relatively happy as you command your Dogo to come to you.

And as with the sit command, give him a little treat the first few times until your Dogo gets itself automatically in the routine of coming when you call him. Do this a few times and it will soon be ingrained in your dog's obedience vocabulary.

Next to teaching your dog to sit down and getting him to come to you, the next most important step in obedience training is to teach your Dogo to drop items on command.

Because Dogos are curious animals, and just like a child they love to pick things up, as a consequence, many undesirable things can wind up in your Dogos mouth. So let's teach him to get rid of them!

For this teaching exercise, we have to get a little bit creative and find something that your Dogo really wants, something that he just loves putting into his mouth and then consciously makes him resist it.

This can be done with a favorite chew toy. It may seem a bit deceptive, but throw his chew toy on the ground as if you are letting him have it. Then, as soon as he comes up to it, step on it, blocking him from the toy.

ıld have your dog's attention at this point, and he ɔubtedly start whining and pawing at your foot. As he does so, this is your cue to loudly command, "Drop it!" Keep repeating the phrase until your dog stops what he is doing and leaves the item alone.

Once your Dogo stops trying to get the object under your foot, give him a treat. Do this enough times and your Dogo will know you mean business when you make the sounds associated with "Drop it!" and he will instantly drop whatever he has when you use this command!

Teaching Your Dogo Argentino Cachorro "Down" And Putting an end to Separation Anxiety

"Please Don't Go! I Get Worried when You Leave!"

The next command phrase we are going to overview is that of the ever important "Down." Being able to tell a Dogo to get down is of critical importance if you have house guests or if you are around small children. You need to be able to make your Dogo understand when you want him to calm down and take a break.

As discussed previously, Dogos have a lot of energy and as a result, they can develop the bad habit of jumping up excitedly on their owners and others when they greet them.

The Dogo mean no harm by it, it's really just his way of showing he cares, and it's his own misguided way of releasing his separation anxiety.

Although this behavior may be cute and endearing in a puppy, with a full grown Dogo it is just too much to deal with to get nearly knocked to the ground every time your dog wants to say "hi!"

So, let's break him of this habit. We are going to have to get a little bit creative for this training. Since we have already made the observation that your dog tends to use his jumping ability as part of his greeting routine, in order to break him of it, we will have to do it when you are first greeting him for the day.

Many dogs start up their greeting routine as soon as they see your car pull up in the driveway, so be ready, he's probably already jumping by the time your car is parked!

Nevertheless, just stay calm and walk up to the door like normal, when you get to the door don't go in right away, instead just crack your door open a few inches to see what your Dogo is doing.

If the second you make eye contact with your Dogo he starts going berserk and hopping around like a lunatic, while still maintaining eye contact through the crack in the door, command him, "Down!" Then shut the door on him while you are still outside.

After a moment or so, open the door again in the same way, and if he starts acting up when he sees you, shut the door once again repeating your command. This is sending a direct message to your Dogo that you will not come inside until he calms down and stops jumping.

Do this as many times as you need until the dog gets the idea. Your dog wants you to come inside and see him so desperately it probably won't take too long before he gets the idea and will calm himself down just to get you to stop peeking in at him and shutting the door!

If after you come inside your Dogo randomly starts to act up again all you have to do is command him, "Down!" The words that he now associates most with the act of calming down will make him calm.

He now associates this word "Down" with the training exercise he just experienced at the door. So just keep reminding him with this command, and you will have one peaceful Dogo.

Many Dogo Argentinos suffer from some form of separation anxiety. No Dogo likes to be alone for extended periods of time and almost every dog, no doubt, displays some level of displeasure. Some may have very mild separation anxiety and simply whine and quietly pout in the corner while you are gone.

On the other extreme, however, the rambunctious Dogo may tear the house apart, chewing up furniture and otherwise wreck the house for you before you get home. Your dog is not being malicious in either case, he is just feeling overwhelmed and does not know how to express his frustration.

But no matter how your Dogo responds to your absence, you must resist the urge of being triggered into a reaction. Because as heartbreaking as your Dogos little cries for attention might be, you can't be let yourself be swayed by them. Because the second you give in and respond to his cries for attention, this only serves to reinforce the Dogos bad behavior.

In order to keep wraps on his separation anxiety in the future, make sure that you keep all of your exits and entrances as nonchalant as possible, try not to make a big show of going out the door.

Instead of making a big deal of it, you should try distracting your dog before you go out by giving him some kind of treat and then as soon as he stops paying attention to you step out the door.

Some think that this kind of sleight of hand, bait and switch maneuver, is somehow cruel. But it really isn't. This little bit of sleight of hand just is a means to makes separation easier for both of you.

Because if you take the time to give your dog a more marked goodbye all its going to do is make him upset, and the more dramatic and prolonged you make your exit the even more upset that he will get. And, that will suddenly attach some sort of significance to your departure.

If you don't draw any attention at all to your exit, your Dogo will assume that you will be right back and not think so much of it. For all he knows your just out checking the mail.

It's just the way a dog's psychology works, if you make dramatic exit the dog responds with drama, but if you leave like it's no big deal, your Dogo will, for the most part, respond in kind.

Just try to keep your actions as low-key as you can, and your Dogos separation anxiety will quickly become a thing of the past. Because any animal acting out like this is simply practicing a behavior it has learned over time.

So as bad as he may be right now, just take some solace in the fact that, if your Dogo learned to react so badly, he can just as easily unlearn it too.

It just takes a bit of time, perseverance, and positive reinforcement, but through your efforts and a bit of trial and error you can put an end to Separation Anxiety.

Diffusing Bad Argentina Dogo Bark!

The Dogo Argentino is known to have a startling and thunderous bark. Fortunately, most Dogos only use their barking apparatus when it is needed, such as to alert you to a prowler trying to break into your house. But, of course, even though these dogs are not usually known as excessive barkers, there is always an exception to the rule.

So, if you do find your Dogo going berserk barking for no apparent reason, there are a few options for you to correct this. The fastest way to neutralize a dog's bark is to keep him busy. Some dogs bark out of sheer boredom, so perhaps just need to engage his attention span and get his mind onto something else.

Chew toys and bones are the perfect candidates for this since they will take up a dog's entire undivided attention as well as instantly remove his bark from the equation since most dogs can't bark and chew at the same time.

This way you can, literally, throw your dog a bone when he is about to bark or even head him off completely by just handing him the bone or chew toy whenever he is usually tempted to bark the most.

That way if he tends to have a barking fit at noon when the mailman swings by the house, then deposit your Dogos chew toy at 11:55 so that your dog is too busy to go postal on the postman.

This method typically is only a short term solution, since you are simply treating the symptoms of the dogs barking and not the root cause of it. This kind strategy only tends to forestall the inevitable until the bad barking Dogo starts up again.

In order to make a long-term modification in the bad barking Dogos behavior, you will have to teach your dog the "quiet" command. Before you command your dog to be quiet, you should allow him to bark around 3 or 4 times but if he goes over the "4 bark limit" then you should intervene and command the Dogo to be "Quiet!"

This way you know that you are not stifling his normal dog responses, you are not rendering him unable to make a sound, but you are reinforcing that his barking must be within controlled limits.

If you are having trouble getting your Dogo to comply to you just your voice command, you can strengthen it through simultaneous secondary stimulus. This might be something like a can filled with coins, or even sprinkling water lightly on his snout as you order, "Quiet!"

Working almost like a benign form of shock treatment, after a while your dog will be conditioned to quiet down as soon as he hears the can shake or feels a drop of water on his muzzle.

If, however, you are still having a difficult time of getting the control of your Dogos bark you might want to explore what options exist with "corrective" collars.

One collar on the market called the "Citronella Collar" has basically the same working premise as the idea of you sprinkling water on your dog's nose. The collar has a built-in microphone and every time your dog barks the microphone picks up the sound, and it triggers a small device in the collar to squirt out citronella on your dog, letting him know that he needs to stop that barking.

This kind of corrective collar is generally viewed as fairly humane, but it has been criticized for the fact that it sometimes goes off from another external stimulus besides your dog's bark. Other dog's barking in a nearby radius has been known to set the collar off, causing the poor Dogo to get sprayed with citronella when he wasn't doing anything wrong.

This obviously defeats the purpose of the collar, but these reports are few and far between, however. Most of the studies on this type of collar have been proven to be effective. If, however, you have concerns about the use of such a device you should always consult your veterinarian before you decide to begin their use.

Teaching Your Dogo Argentino to "Heel" and Walk in Obedience!

If you do have a Dogo that is relatively prone to excitement, another excellent obedience trick that you should teach your Dogo, especially when you are taking it outside for a long walk, is that of the tried and true "Heel" command.

What exactly is "Heel" command, you may be wondering? Getting a dog to heel basically means getting it to slow down, and calm down enough to walk beside you when you have it on a leash.

This command is absolutely essential if you have a dog that is constantly jerking you forward and pulling on the leash. When you tell your dog to "Heel" he should realize that it means to chill out, slow down his pace and walk beside you instead of pulling out ahead of you all the time. There is no reason why you should have to run a marathon every time you walk your dog.

Walking a dog is all about rhythm and coordination and many owners never get this right. A fact that I saw demonstrated with stunning absurdity on the news the other night. I couldn't believe what I was seeing. Apparently, a dog owner had received a citation from the police for walking her dog while she drove her car.

Yep, that's right; the woman was cruising along at 20 to 25 miles an hour while holding her dog's leash out the window of her car as the crazy animal ran to keep up. What was the lady's excuse for this bizarre behavior? She said it was the only way she could keep up with her out of control dog!

So yes, instead of resorting to something bizarre, stupid, or dangerous, you really need to learn how to walk in tandem with your dog and teach them how to heel. This is yet another lesson in obedience that your Dogo should learn early on. Prevent the formation of bad habits by making the guided walk is a part of your dog's routine.

This exercise is best taught with the leash in hand as you walk your Dogo. So, in order to teach him "Heel" just take him out like you normally would, and when your dog begins to pull in front of you pull the leash up slightly bringing the dog closer the heel of your shoe.

If the dog resists, pull more forcefully and command him, "Heel!" as you bring the dog once again to a pace walking beside you. Do this a few times and soon your Dogo will come to a walking pace beside you without having to be pulled on the leash, when he accomplishes this feat be sure to lavish him with praise, telling him, "Good dog!" But do not stop to pet him or otherwise interfere with the walk in the process.

"Heel" is an excellent command for your energetic Dogo to learn, and one that is particularly useful when you are at the park, and your Dogo sees a squirrel or some other small and furry animal he wants to pounce on.

In these instances, the "Heel" command is your lifeline! In order to prevent a disaster, just tighten up on your leash and tell that Dogo to "Heel!" That way you truly can master your Argentino Mastiff and teach your Dogo some obedience!

"No… I'm Not Crazy… I just Look that Way!"

Chapter 6-How To Keep Your Dogo Healthy

From "Dogo Argentino For Sale" to First Checkup

Dogs, just like people, need to be cared for, and they need to have a checkup every once in a while. Even if the breeder swore by your dog's pedigree and gave you a health guarantee, you should still have your Dogo in for checkups starting as a pup and continuing through adulthood.

Most Dogos are born with intestinal parasites such as worms, so in order for your dog to be at its healthiest, it is vital to have your veterinarian start your Dogo on a program to rid them of parasites. The most common internal parasite is that of a roundworm.

Roundworms are detected when a stool sample is given over for laboratory examination. Once worms such as these are identified, the first round treatment for parasites will begin. A special treatment is introduced that eliminates all of the adult worms living in your Dogo.

Then, usually, ten days after this first round, your veterinarian will introduce a second treatment that is intended to wipe out any eggs that were left behind, eliminating them before they can hatch. This should be enough to get rid of these pests for good. But your Dogo will require periodic checkups for the rest of its life to make sure parasites don't ever return.

Parasite control programs should begin by the time your Dogo is two weeks of age. Regular vaccinations should start at about 8 weeks of age. If you have any questions about locating a veterinarian you can always consult with a breeder since they no doubt have a short list of the best canine health care providers in your area.

Once you find a good Vet, the next thing you should focus on is making sure that your Dogo is comfortable with the office visit. You want to make the trip to the Vet as positive of an experience as you can. You want it to be something that your Dogo can look forward to and not dread. Be sure to reward his patient compliance at the Vet's office with your praise.

Establishing Routine with your Argentinian Dogo and his Vet Visits.

After your Dogos first visit to your veterinarian, you should set up a regular schedule for necessary vaccinations and physical examinations. If you establish this routine early, the better off your Dogo will be.

For your first visit be sure to bring any record of previous health and inoculation documents with you to add to your Dogos new Veterinarian's database. As always knowledge is power and the more that you and your Vet know about the health of your Dogo the better.

Vaccinations may be given on an annual basis in the form of booster shots, or to simplify the process, you can have your Dogo take what is known as a "multivalent" vaccine that combines multiple vaccinations into one single shot.

One thing that you should keep in mind, however, before you give your Dogo any vaccine is what the actual risk is of your animal getting the illness you are trying to protect it. Yes, it is a sad conundrum, but one that does happen from time to time.

So if the risk of contracting a certain illness is next to none, you may want to forego that vaccination and focus on inoculating your Dogo against more credible risks instead.

Of primary concern when it comes to vaccinations, your Dogo should at the very least receive vaccines for rabies, hepatitis, and parvovirus since these are known to be especially deadly.

Your Dogo Argentino Puppy and his Dental Health.

Along with necessary vaccinations, as your Dogo ages, you should also start thinking about his dental health. Dental health examinations usually begin when the dog is about 6 months old because it is at this age that your Dogo will have mostly grown in his adult pair of teeth.

Many dog owners focus on the dog's general physical health and yet forget to take care of their dog's teeth. They usually tend to view their dog's health from a general perspective thinking that aspects such as dental care are mere aesthetics.

This is a bad mistake, though, since most dogs whose teeth are left uncared for will wind up with a bad case of periodontal disease by the time they are 4 years old. Teeth need to be regularly cleaned to prevent damage to your dog's gums, and along with regular dental checkups with your Vet, your Dogo should have regular teeth cleaning regimen in place at home.

Like with most routines, it is best if you start cleaning your Dogos teeth while he is still young to be conditioned since the days of being a puppy. It is much harder to introduce the idea of poking around in an adult dog's mouth, so get him used to a toothbrush early on.

A regular soft toothbrush works just fine; there are also specialized "canine" toothbrushes that are a little easier to use since they are specifically designed for a dog. These can be purchased at most pet stores, but in the end, a regular toothbrush will get the job done.

Just make sure that your dog is relaxed and receptive to you when you begin brushing, so they don't suddenly jerk away from you and cause possible injury to themselves in doing so. Even though it is to his benefit, your dog will most likely be a little nervous the first time you try to clean his teeth. So try to reassure him as best you can during the process.

As mentioned, a regular household toothbrush can work just fine. But one thing that you do want to make sure you steer clear of toothpaste designed for humans. This is because many of the brands that people use can be hazardous to a dog if swallowed.

It is for this reason that it is highly recommended that you purchase a dog-specific toothpaste. Along with being safer, the toothpaste for dogs is also more attractive to them, often laced with the scent and taste of chicken, beef, or seafood.

This way, the practice of oral hygiene is somewhat appealing to your animal. If your animal is persistently resistant to the toothbrush, however, there is another option for manual cleaning. You can use dental hygiene pads for dogs.

These are available at most pet stores and are fairly straightforward to use. Just pull your dog's lips apart and start wiping your dog's teeth with the pads, that way you will at least be able to break away most of the bacteria and food lining your Dogos teeth.

Keeping Your Dogo Trimmed and Groomed

Another health habit that should not be neglected is trimming your Dogos nails. The nails on an Dogo Argentino grow very fast and should be trimmed about every two weeks. If you don't trim your Dogos nails, they pose the risk of getting caught on the carpet, blankets, and other household items, causing possible injury to your Dogo as he tries to break free from his ensnarement.

If the nails get too long, it can also make it much more cumbersome for your Dogo to walk, causing him pain. If the nails are neglected long enough, the Dogo will undoubtedly attempt to trim them himself by biting and gnawing at them.

But the result of these attempts at self-trimming is not going to be good since they will most likely lead to further problems and damage. This includes uneven, split, and hang nails caused by your Dogos ineffective attempts to bite his nails down to size.

It may seem strange that an animal would be so reliant on humans for such a basic measure such as trimming his nails, but many years of selective breeding has led to this result. And it truly is best for both you and your Dogo to have a human being trim his nails for him.

If you aren't keen on doing it yourself, you should contact your Vet. They will most probably trim your Dogos nails right there at the vet's office. Another option is using a local dog groomer.

But if you do not wish for the repeated visits to the vet or the groomer to give your doggy a pedicure your best bet is to learn how to trim his nails yourself. If you do decide to trim your Dogos nails yourself just make sure that you have a good trimmer, for the Dogo the scissor style variety seems to work best.

With this kind of clipper just place your dog's nail in between the two blades and squeeze the two handles together to trim the nail. Be sure to have a good styptic powder on hand too just in case you accidentally cut a bit too close, so you can stop any bleeding. It would also be a good idea to have some treats on hand so you can reward your Dogo for his good cooperation in the task.

Much less of a challenge than trimming your Dogos nails, is taking care of your Dogos shiny white coat. Since the Dogos coat is relatively short and has no undercoat to speak of, grooming should be fairly straightforward. A simply brush job twice a week is usually all your Dogo will need.

The only hang up that a Dogo has in this department is his sensitive skin. Because your Dogos skin is often prone to allergies and irritation, always be cognizant of this when you bathe him. Always use a gentle shampoo designed for dogs. Also keep in mind that your Dogos sensitivity extends to prolonged sunlight as well.

The Dogo owner must be aware that their Dogo was just not designed to sit in the sun for very long. His skin tends to sunburn easily. So, if you are taking him on a prolonged outing, be sure to apply some sun block. Many first time owners are surprised to have to apply sun block to a dog, but this is an artifact of the selective breeding process, and skin sensitivity is a standout feature of the breed.

Another more controversial standout, if not an inborn feature of the Dogo is the condition of his ears. As you may have already realized, the pointy upright ears typical of the Dogo standard are not exactly the ears that your Dogo was born with. The Dogo is a breed that has always been subjected to the practice of ear cropping.

The reason for this cropping stems back to when the Dogo was exclusively used as a hunting dog, and the breeders were adamant that having short upright ears was to their benefit.

It was claimed that it not only made the Dogo hear better but also protected him from having other animals biting his ears. What would have otherwise been floppy and hanging ears, and possibly causing injury to the dog were thus cropped.

It has also been claimed that ear cropping lowers infection since it opens up the ear more to the air, but none of these theories have been proven. The Dogo is no longer in vogue as a hunting dog, and any reported cases of animals

ually having floppy ears bitten off by prey are few and far between.

And while proponents of ear cropping try to state its benefits, detractors persistently proclaim that cropping a dog's ears for any reason is nothing short of animal cruelty. Whole movements of animal rights organizations that have been created just to combat what they view as an unjust practice.

Having that said, however, ear cropping done under the right circumstances, is still perfectly legal in the United States, and it is an approved practice by the American Kennel Club. The recommended age for cropping a Dogos ears is at 10-12 weeks old. During the procedure, your animal should be adequately sedated, so he does not feel any pain.

The veterinarian performing the procedure will place marks on your dog's ears indicating where he will make his incision. He will then proceed to cut away 2/3 of the dog's earflap. After this removal, your veterinarian will then work to seal up the edges of the ear where the tissue was removed and stitch the skin together.

The next stage of the operation is when your vet takes out an inverted paper cup, or an aluminum type of rack, and places it on the remaining 1/3 of your dog's ears so that they will stand up in place. This makeshift structure serves to form the iconic shape that the Dogo Argentino's ears are known for.

This kind of shaping tool will remain on your dog's head for about 21 days after the surgery. During your Dogos recovery time, you should be sure to clean out his ears at least once a day in order to prevent the onset of any kind of infection.

As you can see cropping a dog's ear is no minor task, and after hearing of just how much of an ordeal it is, for both you and your Dogo, many have chosen not do go through with it. This technique is however still a part of the breed standard, and if it is done appropriately, you are fully within regulation to do it.

Just take some time to think about what would be best for you and your Dogo, before you do it. The maintenance of your Dogos health is an everyday occurrence. If you are contemplating cropping his ears, finding a good groomer or anything else, you should have at least a minimal amount of knowledge and understanding to be able to help keep your Dogo clean, trimmed, and groomed.

Helping your Dogo Argentino Fight those Pesky Pests!

Yes, unfortunately, all animals have them from time to time. Whether it's fleas, ticks, or mites, unless your Dogo lives in a sterile laboratory somewhere, he is bound to get contaminated with these little buggers from time to time! The most common parasitic nuisance that your Dogo will face is the common flea.

Fleas are much more widespread than we would like to admit. If you go outside, they are everywhere; and if you are low to the ground like our Dogo is, you are exceptionally prone to having them hop on board. The flea is also so tiny that it is barely noticed until infestation occurs.

An adult flea is just barely visible to the naked eye, and if they are sitting perfectly still in your Dogos fur, you may not see them at all. Before a flea reaches adulthood they can be even harder to see. Just prior to becoming an adult a flea passes through three stages; egg, larva, and pupa.

In its larva and pupa stage, the flea is so tiny it is basically microscopic, they are so small that the human eye can only register them when they are a fully grown adult. So, since we don't typically see them in their younger states, most flea treatment is aimed at the fully grown adults.

An infestation results from egg laying; however, since fleas can lay eggs an astonishing 20 times a day, your Dogo can be overrun in no time. As horrible as it sounds these eggs cling to your Dogos hair after they are laid. Yet another reason to be cautious when petting dogs you don't know, because you may unwittingly transfer clinging flea egg's from one dog to another in the process.

The eggs will eventually fall from the dog's hair, and either remains stuck to your Dogos body or drop to the floor of your home where they will soon hatch out into larvae. This whole process happens within about a week after your Dogos initial infestation.

Larvae, for the most part, are immobile and will stay where they fell only traveling a few inches at most from the spot that they were dropped. Despite what you may think, fleas are not born sucking blood. In fact, during the initial larvae stage, a flea is more likely to live on dead organic matter such as dead skin and even fecal matter. (Absolutely lovely right?)

Well, after about a week of munching on dead skin—and God knows what else—your larvae will morph into the protective "pupae" stage. These pupae will then remain dormant until certain stimulus activates them, such as nearby body heat or even the pressure of being stepped on.

These are the indicators that fleas use to know that a host is nearby so that they can hop on board and get ready to begin feeding off of them. Having all of that said, the best way to treat these pesky pests is to take a bit of a holistic approach and take a full inventory of your Dogos environment.

So instead of just treating your Dogo you should treat where your Dogo goes, such as the carpets, and furniture. You should treat these most frequented areas with what is termed an IGR, (Insect Growth Regulator). These are good for wiping out all of those nasty eggs.

To get rid of the adult fleas that have already hatched out, you should use a common over the counter insecticide to blast those little insects into oblivion. Flea collars and flea combs are also suitable for continual prevention of infestation. Besides these proactive treatments, just basic grooming and cleaning of your Dogos fur will work as a great deterrent against these pests.

Along with fleas, another immense nuisance is that of ticks. Though not quite as common as fleas, ticks can become a major problem if you are not careful, and they can be a true nightmare to get rid of.

Ticks jump on their host and dig their sharply pointed "proboscis" or face deep down into their victim's skin. Yes, I know, it is totally disgusting, but this thing actually bores its head into the flesh of its host and once there it will feast on your Dogos blood until someone gets it out.

Worst of all, there are several debilitating illnesses that a Dogo can get from this parasite such as Lyme's disease. Ticks live in much the same places that fleas are found. Fortunately, they are not quite as numerous. But unlike fleas, it only takes one tick to totally ruin your day. The best way to get rid of a tick is to pull it out with tweezers or some similar device.

You also have to be very careful when you are pulling this bad boy out, because if not done right you may cause the tick to clamp down even harder and bury its head even deeper into your Dogos flesh.

If this happens, you will probably pull the body of the tick out, but the head will break off inside your dog creating a horrible chance for infection. If you are unsure about your ability to remove the tick, be sure and contact your veterinarian, they have more than ample resources to successfully remove ticks.

Now, last but not least, on our list of Dogo nasties is that of the mite. They are even harder to treat than fleas. These are completely microscopic. They can also be quite an itchy nuisance and seem to cause more grief to dogs then even fleas do. In fact, one of the most dreaded of canine skin conditions, "mange" is a direct result of the microscopic infestation of mites.

Unfortunately, in many cases a Dogo is born with this kind of condition as the mites can be passed on from their mother. If you are worried that this may be the case, be sure to check the puppy's muzzle. The muzzle is the most common repository of these pests at birth. Also be sure to ask your veterinarian for a topical treatment that you can use to get rid mites. These are just a few ways to get the best of those pesky pests!

Basic First Aid For Your Dogo!

For minor illness or injury, you should be able to deliver some modicum of first aid on site; you shouldn't have to wait on a Veterinarian. In doing this, you should always keep a small, dog version, of a first aid kit around in order to treat your animal in an emergency.

This kit should have all of the First Aid basics. It should include medicated powder, styptic powder, sterilizing alcohol, hydrogen peroxide, gauze bandages, adhesive tape and a dog approved rectal thermometer.

Having a working thermometer available is vital if your dog starts to display signs of illness because it is the temperature that gives you your first snapshot as to what the animal's internal condition is. A normal reading, the standard that you should base his health on, is always going to be around 101 degrees Fahrenheit / 38 degrees Centigrade.

A temperature that reaches higher than this standard, coupled with the classic signs of dull eyes and a warm or a runny nose are all hallmarks of sickness. In order to take your dog's temperature, take a rectal thermometer and lubricate the insertion point with some petroleum jelly so that you can put the thermometer inside the Dogo nice and easy.

Hold the thermometer in place to avoid the dog from pulling the thermometer further inside its rectum and to keep it from falling out. Once you get an accurate reading, gently pull the thermometer out, clean and sanitize it with alcohol, and put it back in your first aid kit for later use. If your dog's temperature exceeds 104 degrees, you should take him to a Vet for treatment immediately.

Administering Medication

There are many times that you may need to give your Dogo medicine. There are primarily two forms that Veterinary medication come in, either in liquid or pill form. To give your Dogo liquid medication, you should grab hold of your Dogos muzzle and then gently pull the lips apart on one side of his mouth.

You can then let the liquid medicine gently trickle through the Dogos teeth. You never want to pour medicine directly down a Dogos throat as he might choke, or even worse, actually inhale the medicine into his lungs putting him at risk for pneumonia.

So be very careful to avoid this by slowly letting the medicine drip through the side of your Dogos teeth. Remain at the dog's side while doing this to keep him calm and to make sure that he does not cough and inadvertently spray you with the medicine.

If your dog struggles with liquid medication, you can also try giving him his medication in pill form. To administer a pill to your Dogo, you are going to have to grab hold of his muzzle and gently pry open his mouth, and with his head slightly back, place the pill capsule far back on the Dogos tongue.

Now put the palm of your hand over your dog's muzzle and one side of his jaw, with your thumb on the other side. Try to press his lips hard against his teeth while using your other hand to bring down his lower jaw. Keep his mouth closed and this should force the Dogo to have to swallow the medicine.

Talk about a tough pill to swallow, but in reality, it is always an ordeal for a dog to swallow a pill, so try to be as gentle and comforting as you can in the process. Stroke his neck and comfort him while you do this and once he does swallow the pill, try to keep an eye on him to make sure that he doesn't throw up or spit it out after swallowing.

Insuring Your Dogo for Life

To ensure your animal's health for the long run, preferably while he is still a puppy and certainly before your Dogo gets very old, you should think about investing in his health by purchasing his own health insurance. Known as "Pet Insurance" you should be able to take out a fairly cost effective policy.

Such a policy could prove to be essential if your animal happens to have been born with a genetic abnormality. The most common abnormality that most Dogos face is that of being born deaf. About 10% of all Argentino Dogos are born without any use of their sense of hearing.

If this is the case for your Dogo, and you have a big enough heart to see your dog through his disability, then you most definitely need to have proper veterinary treatment established. Your Dogos condition will need to be monitored.

The Dogo Argentino is an impressive but demanding animal even at its healthiest. Be sure to respect his needs by making a serious effort to maintain his health. Keep your Dogo healthy and happy for life.

Chapter 7-Dogo Argentino Breeders; What To Know And What To Expect.

"I had the strangest dream...
I was a puppy, and I was sleeping
with these other...
Oh, wait...Never mind!"

Finding and Preparing for Your Dogo Dog Breeder

Many potential dog buyers are not quite prepared to do their homework before they visit a breeder. As a result, they find themselves in the midst of some hasty decision-making when they are looking into those cute puppy dog eyes.

But while cuteness is a definite plus, you should try asking around with some other dog professionals before you make a deal with the first breeder you come in contact with.

And the first dog professional you should consult in this would be your local Veterinarian. As mentioned in the previous chapter, the Vet is always going to have a database of good contacts at their disposal.

You can also make an effort to contact local dog clubs that specialize in Dogo Argentino breeds such as the American Kennel Club and a variety of other dog breeding associations.

It is by using a reputable breeder that you get can get some sense of security on your Dogos future health, personality, and what his general appearance and disposition will be when he gets a little older.

Upon selecting your breeder, you should go with the one with consistently high ratings. A good reputation is worth its weight in gold when it comes to Dogos Argentinos so don't hesitate to search for a reputable breeder.

Dog shows are another great place to find potential breeders. Most people who participate in such shows are breeders themselves, and it couldn't be easier to know which ones are the best breeders in this instance because all you have to do is see how many trophies they've won in order to see just how good they are.

No matter where you find your breeder, however, when you go to a breeder, just keep in mind that you get what you pay for. Prices range from $500 all the way to $2,000 (€450 to €1,800) for a Dogo Argentino. There are reasons for the fluctuation in cost.

I'm not saying that it is impossible to get a "good deal" on your Dogo, but if you are browsing for Dogos on the lower price range just be cautious, and be sure that you thoroughly check the puppy for any defects that the breeder may be trying to hide from you.

It would also be wise to keep in mind that just because your Dogo is a verified as a purebred dog, it does not necessarily guarantee the health and physical characteristics of the puppy. There can always be unforeseen genetic factors down the road, so be prepared just in case the unexpected may occur.

The Breed Standard of the Dogo Argentino

Always be sure to consult the "breed standard" before you make a purchase. The breed standard just as the name implies; is the standard ingredients that make up a particular breed of dog, explicitly highlighting the ideal mental and physical dispositions of the dog.

When it comes to the Dogo Argentino, the breed standard goes back to its creator Dr. Antonio Nores Martinez, which he officially published in 1947.

According to Antonio's official breed standard, the Dogo Argentino should be "harmonically beautiful" meaning that the dog should maintain a harmonic balance between its appearance and its ability to perform the general tasks that the breed was created for, such as hunting, guarding, and the like.

Antonio also emphatically stated that the Dogo Argentino "is the only white, short-haired dog of its size and weight" which is able to perform such role-specific tasks so well, and is the only dog of its size and coloring that is strong enough to be able to subdue large animals as was the case with Antonio's original intention of using the Dogo to take out the wild South American Boar.

So in order for this breed standard to be correct, the dog's size, coloring, strength, and ability had to match up to the original blueprint it was designed with.

The temperament and intelligence of the Dogo are also an integral part of this dog's breed standard. Under normal conditions, the Dogo Argentino is a very clever animal. It was designed that way with its original purpose as a hunting dog. It was specifically built with the capacity to outsmart its prey.

Through persistent trial and error, Antonio created a very intelligent animal, and it is considered a fault of the breed standard if the dog appears to show lower than normal intelligence.

While canine IQ isn't factored into the equation with most other breeds, for this exceptional dog brains do matter, creating a very smart dog and a very smart standard for the Dogo Argentino.

Fact Checking Your Dogos Pedigree

When you buy your Dogo from a local breeder you should be supplied with a complete "pedigree" this means that you receive a complete written record of your Dogos ancestry going back at least three generations.

You probably didn't think the grandpa of your Dogo would matter much, but if the breeder is a professional, they will have the performance traits and characteristics of all the dogs in your pup's background going back at least to the third generation if not further.

Upon purchasing your Dogo, your breeder should provide you with an official—and completely filled out—registration application for your Dogo. And while doing this, you should also look into "pet insurance". As mentioned in the previous chapter, having a good policy for pet insurance is a great guarantee on your Dogos future health.

A suitable insurance policy can serve to cover you and your dog if your animal is somehow injured, accidentally poisoned, or if it suffers from any of a whole host of medical conditions.

Everyone loves a purebred dog such as the Dogo Argentino, and breeders swear by his or her reliability and temperament. But don't just take their word for it, when you meet with a breeder be sure to ask them if they have done any specific genetic and health testing. Any breeder who is truly invested in the health of their animals will have at least some basic testing done on their dogs.

Most importantly they should have conducted testing to determine if the puppies are at risk for basic structural ailments such as hip and elbow dysplasia, a disorder that can lead to a crippled dog later in life.

In order to make sure that your pup is healthy and happy, be sure to ask the breeder about these testing procedures. Most will be more than glad to comply, and may even give you personal records including x-rays indicating that the Dogo cleared certain testing for structural abnormalities.

A good breeder has no fear of screening because they have confidence in their own breeding practices to reduce the chance of any possible inheriting of genetic disorders. They have so much invested in the Dogo Argentino's health that they know exactly what kind of animal that they are breeding.

This is the difference between a true breeder and the more notorious puppy mills that produce dogs just for sheer profit and do not care about the actual well-being of the animals. Because it is the puppy mill that spends the least amount of time and money on the health of their dogs in order to maximize their profits.

A good breeder, on the other hand, is more than willing to spend a good chunk of their energy and finances in order to produce a healthy animal. Not only that, a truly compassionate breeder will often make it a point to stay involved with their clients long after the sale is made.

Developing a Lasting Relationship with Your Breeder

Many responsible, caring breeders wind up maintaining communication with their clients, offering their support, and advice in raising the Dogo pups they sold you. Truly considerate breeders also sell their animals with neuter and spay contracts, a clear indication that they care about the Dogos future in the long run.

Most breeders do not usually go out of their way to advertise themselves, and much of their business is through word of mouth and repeat clients. Having said that however if you do enough digging on the internet and at local dog show events, you should be able to find some good breeders in your area.

And as we mentioned in the chapter about purchasing Dogos, the American Kennel club is always going to be an invaluable resource. So feel free to pay them a visit at http://www.akc.org. Still, however you locate your breeder, just try and make sure that the folks that bred your Dogo, loved your Dogo Argentino as much as you will.

Dogo Argentino Rescue: The Breeder Alternative

While a Rescue Service and a Breeder are two distinctly different things, the Rescue often serves as a recipient of much of the runoff from some of the less scrupulous Dog Breeders. Many healthy dogs wind up at rescue shelters and services out of no fault of their own.

So, if you have a big heart and would love to get one of the pups at your local rescue, giving it a chance for a loving home … don't hesitate. Because there are many high-quality Dogos that were simply dealt a bad hand from their breeder and wound up in the rescue circuit. If you find that's the case, don't hesitate to give these wonderful dogs a home.

"Just Look at these Eyes!
Who Could Say No?"

Chapter 8-Argentina Dog Leisure! This Dogo Dog Breed Likes To Play!

"Come on Guys! Just Follow me To Playtime!"

Laying Down the Ground Rules for Playtime with your Dogo Puppies

In this book, the things we have talked about may seem like a lot of work; well, now we are going to take a moment to discuss the antithesis-- playtime! But don't be fooled, however, because even directing your dog towards play may require some guidelines. I can feel you rolling your eyes at the page right now as you think, "What? I need a user manual to play with my dog?"

No, it's not quite that intense, and if you have followed the general guidelines in this book so far, especially the chapters on housebreaking and obedience, you are already well on the way. But even playtime needs some ground rules. And one thing is for certain, although when roughhousing in your house anything might go, out in the public arena this is simply not the case.

Especially if you take your dog to the park or other places where multiple people and animals gather, your Dogo needs to understand a certain amount of etiquette when it is playing around others.

As an owner, it is your responsibility to make sure that your dog does not intimidate, harass, attack, or stalk other animals and people when you take him out to play. Your dog needs to learn, early on, that you expect it to respect other people and animals it may encounter—even during its playtime.

While your dog needs to follow the rules, the owner is the first to decide which certain rules may apply. Many owners like to let their dog run loose without a leash for example, but unless a dog park or other recreation area explicitly permits unrestrained dogs, you should make sure your Dogo is on its leash at all times. In this way, obedience begins with the dog owner as he obeys the ordinances of where he takes the dog to play.

As a general rule, an owner who is obedient to the city ordinances and rules of his community is much more likely to produce a dog that is in turn obedient to them. In the end, our dogs look to us for an example and to the guidance-loving Dogo Argentino in particular; he will look to you as his direct pack leader to follow.

An Invitation to Play

Many Dogo owners find that their dog may seem slow or somewhat apprehensive to play, or almost like they don't know how. This is mostly due to the Dogos nature, and in reality, if they seem slow to cut loose, they are most likely waiting for your invitation to do so.

In the dog world, other dog's invite each other to play through their body language, and since your Dogo is looking to you as its lead dog, it's waiting for you to show it a sign that you want to let down your guard and play a little.

If you are overly rigid and serious all the time, your dog will not feel comfortable enough to play. When a dog wants to get another dog to loosen up for playtime, it will wiggle its body and excitedly bark. You may have to hang out close by to verify and permit this canine invite.

Now you may feel a little silly imitating a dog in order to bring out your Dogos playfulness, and you don't have to go too crazy with it. You don't have to get on all fours and bark like a dog.

But, you can at least loosen up a bit, and crouch down near your dog. Start by excitedly encouraging it with playful phrases such as, "Playtime!" and "Who wants to play?" This will also further the dog's command vocabulary, and it will come to understand the meaning behind the phrase "playtime."

The Dogo Argentino Hunting Instinct
and Play Fighting

"Come on buddy! Enough already!
People Are Watching! Either Bite Me or Go Home!
This is Embarrassing!"

Since your Dogo was a puppy he no doubt has desired to express himself in play fighting. He may have engaged in brief little playful battles nipping at his littermates before you adopted him. While your Dogo is in your charge, he still desires this form of expression for his energy.

One of the best ways to allow your dog to play in this fashion is with a game of tug of war. Your Dogo would like nothing more than to tug with one end of the rope in his mouth while you pull with all your might on the other.

Just a regular piece of rope should be fine for this feat, but you can also get many other pet store varieties that should be safe substitutes as well. The most popular tug toy of the Dogo is no doubt rawhide, and this is usually an excellent tool to help them engage in resistance, you just need to be careful to check the specifics on the rawhide ingredients, since some brands are more healthy than others.

These sort of tug of war games are good every once in a while but don't get your dog into the habit of expecting this kind of play all the time. Otherwise, you may get your Dogo so used to chewing and pulling that it becomes all he wants to do, and the next thing know your best pair of leather shoes might become his favorite chew toy! Believe me; it's happened to me before!

So save the tug of war as an irregular game between the two of you to help him relieve occasional aggression, but don't let him get accustomed to playing like this all the time. Keep roughhousing as a rare treat for your Dogo. Also be sure to look out for any overly aggressive signs in your Dogos body language.

You should especially be concerned if your Dogo begins to make direct eye contact with you. Because as much as we may enjoy a sudden look in the eye as human beings and it might be a good thing for our overall business acumen. Your Dogo is still a dog, and he isn't looking you in the eye to pass a job interview.

Dogs just don't normally do that. The only time a dog actively tries to look someone directly in the eye is when they are about to attack. (Sounds like an old boss I had too, but that's a story for another time!)

Besides giving you a stare down, other signs of aggression that you should be particularly concerned with include: "tail standing", "ear-pricking", and "chest puffing".

All of these body language postures indicates that your Dogo is becoming dangerously aggressive, and if you see him engaging with you in such a fashion, it's time to end his play time until he can start acting rationally again.

Unfortunately, as much as we want them to, many just Dogos find it difficult to separate vigorous play from more aggressive actions. Sometimes, it just takes them a little bit of time to figure out the difference. So while you are still feeling out your Dogos personality, it is crucial to heed these warning signs.

Being born with a natural hunting instinct, another game your Dogo always loves to play is that of the chase. Whether it's a ball, a stick, or just an old rolled up sock, anything you throw past your Dogo, he is instinctively going to want to chase and run after. This is a game that your Dogo will never get tired of playing, and you can safely play fetch with him at just about any time of day.

I always enjoy a good game of Frisbee with my Dogo. I just take him to the park and start launching my Frisbee in the air and watch the Dogo go. He absolutely loves chasing it, and I get a kick out of watching his goofy antics as he tries to keep up with it. It's also a great reason to pay a visit to the park to get some exercise the both of us.

These are all good ways to engage your dog in play, but some Dogos have a flat out crazy streak when it comes to playing, and you don't have to do any convincing at all to get them started. The Dogo Argentino is known to get a bit goofy at times when it wants to play and release some energy.

The dog could be either indoors or outdoors and suddenly get that crazy, mischievous look in his eye and start running around in circles. This is a good time to take your Dogo to the park because it is precisely this goofy madness that your Dogo Argentino uses to let you know that it is playtime!

"More, More, MORE!"

Chapter 9- How To Keep That Dogo Argentino Cazando Happy!

The Quick Study; Your Dogos Intelligence.

"My Reference Library is bigger than Yours!"

The temperament of the Dogo is something that we have already touched on briefly throughout this book, but I just wanted to designate one more chapter towards the exact temperament of this breed and what it takes to make this animal happy.

This dog is extremely loyal and a natural guardian of life and property. He is also very intelligent, in fact, *one of the most intelligent*, top ranked on the IQ scale of dogs. This means that the Dogo, when given the right direction, should be a rather quick study, making training this dog all the more enjoyable.

As mentioned previously, the Dogos intelligence is even part of his breed standard, so always keep in mind just how exceptional of an animal your Dogo is when dealing with him. He is very perceptive and can easily pick up on your true emotional and mental states.

So don't try to put one past this Dogo, and do your best to communicate with him honestly and equitably in order to keep him happy. He's one smart puppy so treat him according to his intellect!

What it Takes to Keep Your Dogo Argentino Happy.

It just takes a firm hand and consistent, but loving, authority to keep this Dogo happy. The Dogo Argentino is a generally good natured dog, but they are simply not good for everyone and especially not those that are submissive and shrink from the task of dishing out authority.

Because the Dogo needs to be submissive, it craves it; the dog does not want to be an over-dominant bully in the house, it only opts to do so as a matter of last resort when the owner doesn't step up. Obviously, a dog cannot be the boss of the house and this sad attempt of the dog to take charge in an uncertain environment will ultimately lead to failure.

But the dog doesn't know that; he is just following his instinct to try and lead what he feels is a leaderless pack. Before your Dogo gets any confused ideas about who is in charge, you need to exert your dominance over your dog from day one.

This doesn't mean you have to be overly aggressive yourself; it just means you need to display firm and fair authority over your Dogo. He will thank you for it later.

The Dogo Argentino really just needs people that are firm, confident and consistent in their rulemaking and he will follow without fail. This dog instinctively needs solid rules and regulations, without this firm foundation the dog slides into chaos and experiences severe anxiety from the lack of control in his life.

Correcting Potential Dominance Issues

"Me...Dominate?"

Your Dogo is a natural pack animal, and being such he needs to feel that there is order in his pack. As mentioned previously, the Dogo is smart, and he is a quick study, and he sizes up the rankings of his household at lightning speed.

The danger in this comes when a less authoritative person in his territory appears a bit weak and submissive. This is not a place you want your Dogo to go, and it can lead to some very tricky dominance issues.

Because when it comes to a Dogo living with humans, he needs to realize that humans will always be ahead of him in the pecking order. No person in your household should be deemed by your Dogo as its inferior.

It sounds funny, and many of us have had the experience of someone in our household, maybe a more meek and mild personality in our family, being suddenly pushed around by our Dogo.

But initial comic relief aside, in the long run, it is not right for the Dogo, or your family, to have the dog view any human being as under his charge. M wife and I had our own run in with this kind of wayward Dogo dominance in temperament. At the time we had a male Dogo Argentino and a female Labrador mix.

Both dogs had already been fixed so unwanted pups was not an issue and our Dogo soon took the Lab under his wing as his subordinate protégé. She didn't seem to mind and in their own perceived dog pack, it just appeared to be their natural pecking order. We didn't think much of it, we thought it was kind of cute and even began to nickname our Dogo, "the boss."

But the cuteness wore off when the dog began to expand his bossiness to my wife. The conflict began over his dominance of the Labrador. I was away from the house when the Dogo snapped at my wife. If I was there, I probably would have been relatively angry and reacted badly. But my wife being the much cooler thinking one of the bunch knew what was going on.

She had simply walked over to our Lab to see how she was doing, but the second she began to pat her on the head, our bossy Dogo went nuts and started barking and growling, and before she knew it, he ran over and nipped at her. Fortunately, all he did was graze her sweater, but that was enough to scare the crap out of us.

When I heard about it, I started putting our Dogo in the crate every time I left the house. But this was not a sustainable situation, and we soon felt very sorry for him. We immediately knew what the problem was; our Dogo was so dominating over our other dog that he thought it was his responsibility to keep her in line and his alone.

Unsure of exactly how to proceed we contacted our local veterinarian. After telling her our story, she instructed us to avoid any situation that provoked our Dogo over the next few days. Admittedly, at first this seemed counter-productive as if we were letting the impulsive temperament of our doggy win, but it took an immediate easing of the situation to get our Dogo psychologically ready for the adjustment we were going to deliver.

Once our Dogo had been calm for a while with no reason to be upset or aggressive, we then entered the second phase of the strategy by having both of us cease in our affection toward the Dogo. This may seem a little cruel, but it works trust me.

All you have to do is withhold your usual attention, and this Dogo soon becomes so desperate for your affirmation that he will do anything to get it. This puts him back in the perfect, receptive, temperament to listen to your commands and accept you once again as his
authority figure.

Sorry, Mr. Bossy Doggy but you gotta listen to reason! And he soon did, he was eager to do anything to get on our good side again. And so with our Dogo in this state of compliance, we began to reassert our control over the lab and began to chip away at his perceived dominance.

My wife would go over to her and pet her affectionately and the second our Dogo began to look over with aggression on his mind we would snap, "No! Down!" and when he complied, we would finally shower him with his much sought after attention and praise.

In the end, the Dogo proved to be quite addicted to our affection and quickly decided that being loved was much better than being the boss, and relinquished his attempted coup of the household!

And what does our little story prove? Well, my friends, it shows that your Dogos temperament is what you make it, and you too can make your Dogo a happy perrito with a little bit of patience and perseverance!

"I claim this Land in the name of Dogos Everywhere!"

Dogo Argentino Kennels and Helping Your Dogo Through his Golden Years

"Wow! I can see my house from here!"

After you've established the ground rules with your Dogo, get ready for a long and happy life with your Argentine Mastiff, because this breed can live as long as 15 years. And, as he enters into his golden years as a senior dog you are going to have to start paying a little extra attention to him and his needs.

Technically, a Dogo Argentino is considered to have reached his Golden Years of Seniority when he is about 7 years old. This is the marker that most behaviorists and vets use to classify the Dogo as a senior citizen dog.

And although it won't qualify him for discount haircuts and 50% off at Applebee's, this is a very special time for your Dogo Argentino. This is a time that your dog should be slowing down, and he will need to begin his involvement in "senior care" programs with the veterinarian.

These sessions should include a visit to the Vet every 6 months along with regular screenings that monitor your Dogos overall health. This screen includes lab tests such as urinalysis, blood smears, electrocardiogram, along with regular checks of his blood pressure.

Dogos just like people require a lot of extra work when they get older, and a Dogo extremely advanced in age may eventually need what would equate to an assisted living arrangement in human terms. There are actually many Dog Kennels that provide this resource for elderly dogs.

Ever since your Dogo was a puppy you knew that you had a responsibility to care for him for the rest of his life. Don't give up this commitment just because he gets older. Proper preventative health care for your Dogo will not only help to extend his life but will also ensure that he remains carefree and happy all the way through his Golden Years!

"Thanks for being a loyal friend!"

Conclusion-Like only the Dogo Knows!

The Dogo Argentino just like every other dog on this planet belongs to the rich tapestry that humans and dogs have interwoven in an immense fabric of mutual benefit over the past 10,000 years or so.

The first stage of this unique relationship began when canine ancestors began to follow the nomadic humans of the Ice Age perhaps merely tagging along with hunters to pick up the scraps they left behind.

Their tasks soon evolved beyond just picking up the leftovers. However, they quickly developed new roles.

They became tracking dogs for hunters, protectors of flocks, and companions at home. The fate of man and his dog became inseparable threads of a shared destiny.

In fact, humans and dogs have grown to depend on each other so much that scientists believe that it is our relationship with dogs that has helped to shape the course of our human evolution.

Amazingly even our brain function seems to mirror each other. Studies have proven that the brain waves of dogs and humans are practically identical over a wide range of stressors.

Dogs have the same basic emotions, and the Dogo Argentino, in particular, can be said to be a particularly rare breed of emotionally intelligent animal. With an IQ that hovers around the level of a five-year-old child, it is said that if the Dogos tongue was suitably designed for it, it could actually speak to us!

It may sound strange and even perhaps a bit startling, but the Dogo already has a firm grasp of what several of our commands and phrases mean. The Dogo Argentino has an amazing ability with vocabulary comprehension.

So much so, that I know some Dogo owners that have to spell out certain words they don't want their dog to hear! Seriously! I had a friend with a Dogo that always had to spell out Veterinarian as V—E – T, otherwise if her Dogo heard the magical word when she said, "I've got to talk my dog to the Vet." That Dogo was history!

So just think about it, our Dogo already has a firm grasp of what we are saying. He sits back and intently listens to our beck and call, now just imagine how crazy it would be if it could give you a personal response!

Yeah, I would probably have a heart attack, but just imagine when you are ruffling your Dogos hair telling him, "Oh! You are such a good boy!" that he turns to you and remarks smugly, "Yeah, I know."

That would be great right? (Besides being freakishly bizarre?) Well, believe it or not, thanks to a research team in Sweden, in the near future we may have some dogs fully equipped with basic conversation.

These guys are apparently fashioning out headsets that can read a dog's brainwaves and then translate it into speech. (You know, via one of those Stephen Hawking styled computer voice synthesizers.) That way when your dog sniffs your neighbor's butt, he can tell you exactly how he feels!

Ok, that is going a bit beyond far-fetched! Talking Dogos? I'm not sure if I am ready for that just yet, but as it is, the Dogo Argentino has got to be one of the most rewarding dogs in existence.

It was bred to certain specifications and expectations, and as long as you have some small understanding of this dog breed and some general dog training ability, there is no reason why your experience with the Dogo Argentino wouldn't be a good one.

I hope that this book has given you the direction and confidence that you need to have a wonderful experience with your new Dogo Argentino.

Whether you get your Dogo through a friend, a breeder, a kennel, a pet store or a rescue, you will soon feel the love, pride, and happiness that only an owner of a Dogo Argentino can know!

Thank you for Reading!

Index

***